I Love the

Contents

The United Kingdom

Scotland, Northern Ireland, Wales and England are the four parts of the United Kingdom.

This book tells you about places to visit in the United Kingdom. Where do you want to go?

The Causeway Coast

Snowdonia

Cheddar

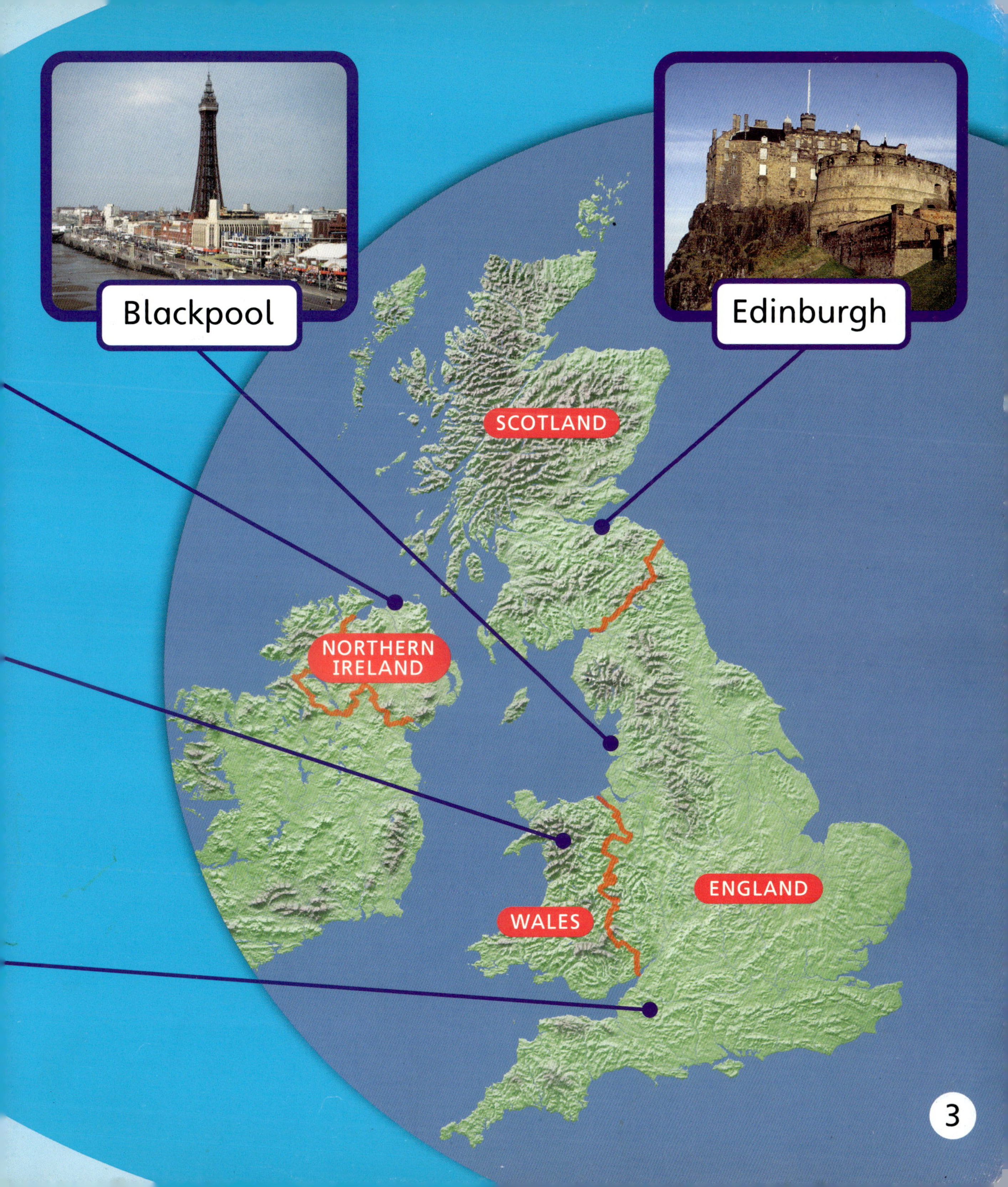
Blackpool
Edinburgh
SCOTLAND
NORTHERN IRELAND
WALES
ENGLAND

Edinburgh

Edinburgh is the capital city of Scotland. There has been a castle in Edinburgh for over 1000 years.

Long ago prisoners were kept in the castle. You can still see where some of them wrote on the walls!

A big gun is fired from the castle, at one o'clock each day. You can hear the bang all over the city.

In Victorian times, a dog called Bobby lived in Edinburgh. After his owner died, Bobby lived by his grave for over fourteen years. This statue was put up in Bobby's memory.

You can see Arthur's Seat from the city centre.
It looks like a hill but it's really an old volcano!

The Royal Yacht *Britannia*, is kept in Edinburgh. *Britannia* used to belong to the Queen. Today you can go aboard and even look inside the Queen's bedroom!

Blackpool

Blackpool is a seaside town in the north of England. Blackpool Tower was built in Victorian times.

Blackpool Tower is more than 150 metres high. You can get to the top of the tower in a lift. On a clear day you can see for miles.

In autumn, the tower and the seafront are lit up with thousands of lights. These lights are called the Illuminations.

Blackpool has miles and miles of sandy beaches. You can play on the sand or ride on a donkey.

Blackpool Pleasure Beach has some of the biggest and scariest rides in the United Kingdom. Millions of people go there every year.

The first sticks of Blackpool rock were made in 1887 by Ben Bullock. Now you can buy rock in many shapes, colours and flavours.

Cheddar

Cheddar is a village in the south of England. Cheddar Gorge has the highest cliffs in England. They are about 130 metres high.

The best way to get to the top of the Gorge is to climb up the 274 steps called Jacob's Ladder.

There are lots of caves in the Gorge. Some of them are open to visitors.

Lots of people go to Cheddar to climb the steep sides of the the Gorge.

You can play a game of crazy golf in Cheddar. There are 18 different holes on the course for you to enjoy.

The village of Cheddar has been famous for its cheese for more than 800 years. Today, you can see the cheese being made.

Snowdonia

Snowdonia is the largest national park in Wales. Snowdon is the highest mountain in Snowdonia.

There are lots of mountain railways in Snowdonia. One of the railways even goes to the top of Snowdon.

Snowdon is also the highest mountain in Wales. It is over 1000 metres high. There is a cafe and a shop at the top!

Mountain biking is very popular in Snowdonia. There are lots of bike trails to go on in the national park.

You can go underground to visit the Victorian copper mines at Sygun. You will need to wear a hard hat!

Portmeirion is an unusual village to visit. It was built by a man as a private village – just for himself! The man died in 1978 and no-one lives there now. But, visitors are still welcome.

The Causeway Coast

The Causeway Coast is by the sea in Northern Ireland. The Giant's Causeway is made up of 40 000 tall rocks.

Legend says that a giant made the causeway, so he could walk to Scotland to fight another giant, without getting his feet wet!

Legend says that this rock is one of the giant's boots!

At Carrick-a-Rede you can walk across this rope bridge. It is 25 metres above the sea and is very wobbly.

You can have fun on the water slides at Waterworld in Portrush.

Dunluce castle sits on the edge of tall cliffs. Hundreds of years ago, part of the castle broke off and the kitchen fell into the sea!

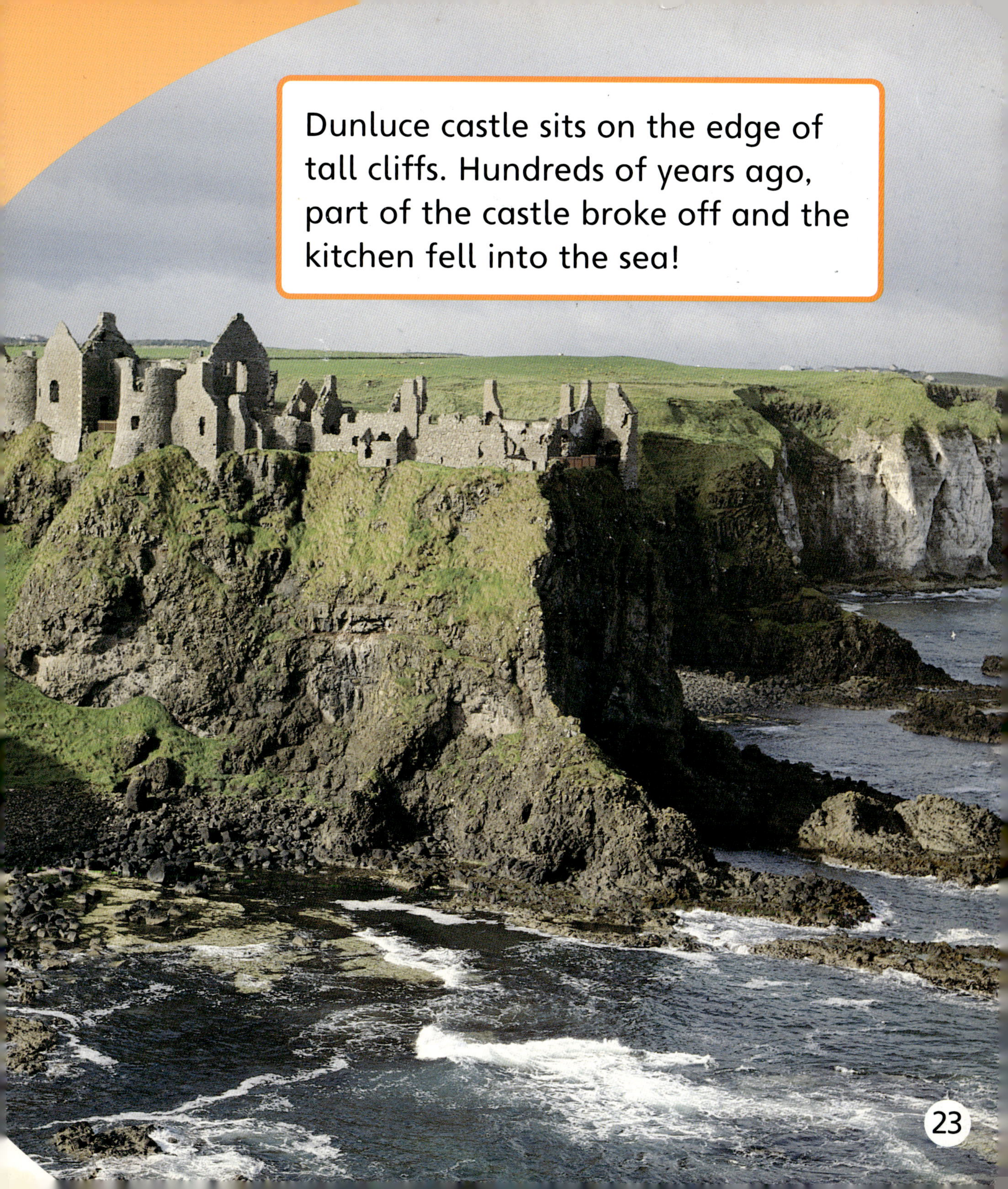

Index